This activity book belongs to:

_____

_____

ă   a

a a a a a a a a

ă   a

a a a a a a a a

ANT

A is for ANT

Ant

Ant Ant Ant Ant

Ant Ant Ant Ant

Practice page

Practice page

b

b

b b b b b b b

B

B

B B B B B B

BEAR

B is For Bear

Bear

Bear   Bear   Bear

bear   bear   bear

Practice page

Practice page

Ć

c

c c c c c c c c c

C

c

c c c c c c c c c

CAT

c is for cat

Cat

Cat Cat Cat

cat cat cat

Practice page

Practice page

LETTER D

d   d

d d d d d d d

D   D

D D D D D D D

DOG

D is for Dog

Dog

Dog Dog Dog

dog dog dog

Practice page

Practice page

Elephant

E is for Elephant

Elephant

Elephant   *Elephant*

elephant   *elephant*

Practice page

Practice page

LETTER f

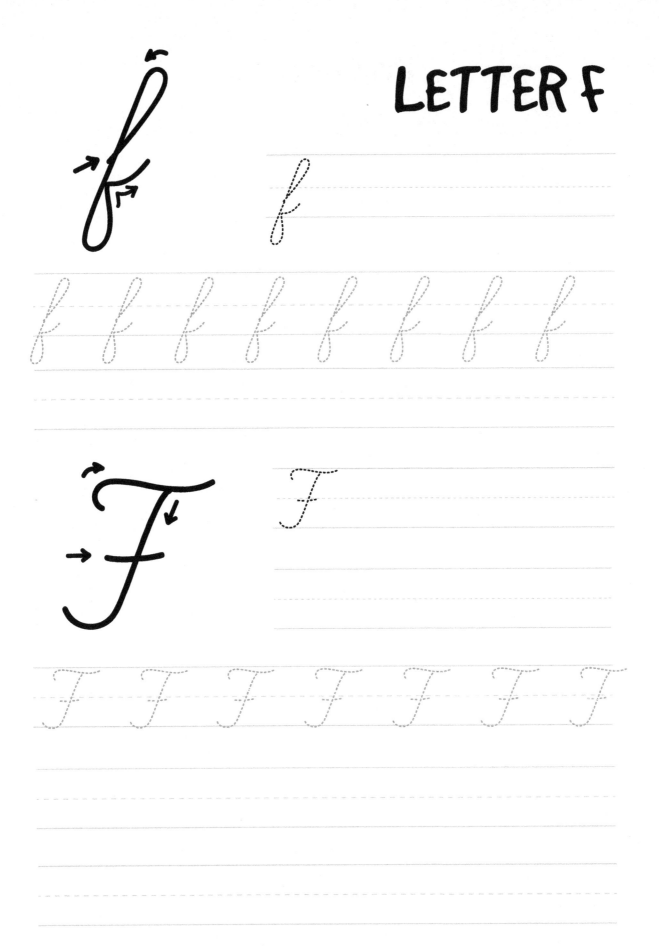

FLAMINGO

F is for flamingo

Flamingo

Flamingo Flamingo

flamingo flamingo

Practice page

Practice page

GIRAFFE

G is for Giraffe

Giraffe

Giraffe   Giraffe

giraffe   giraffe

Practice page

Practice page

h

h h h h h h h

H

H H H H H H H

HIPPOPOTAMUS

H is for Hippopotamus

Hippopotamus

Hippopotamus

hippopotamus

Practice page

Practice page

i

i

i i i i i i i i i

l

l

l l l l l l l

IGUANA

I is for Iguana

Iguana

Iguana Iguana

iguana iguana

Practice page

Practice page

JELLYFISH

J is for Jellyfish

Jellyfish

Jellyfish   Jellyfish

jellyfish   jellyfish

Practice page

Practice page

k

k

k k k k k k k

K

K

K K K K K K K K

KANGAROO

K is for Kangaroo

Kangaroo

Kangaroo

kangaroo

Practice page

Practice page

l

l

l l l l l l l l

L

L

L L L L L L

LION

L is for Lion

Lion

Lion Lion Lion

lion lion lion lion

Practice page

Practice page

$\mathcal{M}$ m

m m m m m

$\mathcal{M}$ m

m m m m m

MOUSE

M is for Mouse

Mouse

Mouse Mouse

mouse mouse

Practice page

Practice page

n

n

n n n n n n n

n

n

n n n n n n

NARWHAL

N is for Narwhal

Narwhal

Narwhal Narwhal

narwhal narwhal

Practice page

Practice page

O

o

o o o o o o o o o o o o o o

O

O

O O O O O O O O O O O O O O

OCTOPUS

O is for octopus

Octopus

Octopus Octopus

octopus octopus

Practice page

Practice page

$\mathcal{P}$ $\mathcal{P}$

$\mathcal{P}$ $\mathcal{P}$ $\mathcal{P}$ $\mathcal{P}$ $\mathcal{P}$ $\mathcal{P}$ $\mathcal{P}$

$\mathcal{P}$ $\mathcal{P}$

$\mathcal{P}$ $\mathcal{P}$ $\mathcal{P}$ $\mathcal{P}$ $\mathcal{P}$ $\mathcal{P}$ $\mathcal{P}$

PIG

P is for Pig

Pig

Pig Pig Pig Pig

pig pig pig pig

Practice page

Practice page

q

q

q q q q q q q

Q

Q

Q Q Q Q Q Q Q

QUAIL

Q is for Quail

Quail

Quail Quail Quail

quail quail quail

Practice page

Practice page

r

r r r r r r r r

R R

R R R R R R R

RABBIT

R is for Rabbit

Rabbit

Rabbit Rabbit

rabbit rabbit

Practice page

Practice page

SNAIL

S is for Snail

Snail

Snail Snail Snail

snail snail snail

Practice page

Practice page

LETTER T

t

t

t   t   t   t   t   t   t   t

T

T

T   T   T   T   T   T   T   T

TURTLE

T is for Turtle

Turtle

Turtle Turtle Turtle

turtle turtle turtle

Practice page

Practice page

$\mathcal{U}$

u

$u \quad u \quad u \quad u \quad u \quad u \quad u$

$\mathcal{U}$

$\mathcal{U}$

$\mathcal{U} \quad \mathcal{U} \quad \mathcal{U} \quad \mathcal{U} \quad \mathcal{U} \quad \mathcal{U}$

UNICORN

U is for Unicorn

Unicorn

Unicorn Unicorn

unicorn unicorn

Practice page

Practice page

$\nearrow \mathcal{U}$

$\mathcal{U}$

$\mathcal{U} \quad \mathcal{U} \quad \mathcal{U} \quad \mathcal{U} \quad \mathcal{U} \quad \mathcal{U}$

$\nearrow \mathcal{V}$

$\mathcal{V}$

$\mathcal{V} \quad \mathcal{V} \quad \mathcal{V} \quad \mathcal{V} \quad \mathcal{V} \quad \mathcal{V} \quad \mathcal{V}$

VULTURE

V is for Vulture

Vulture

Vulture Vulture

vulture vulture

Practice page

Practice page

LETTER W

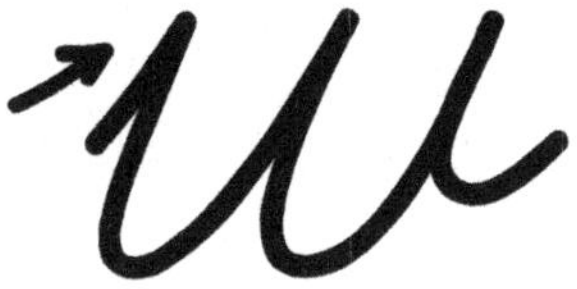

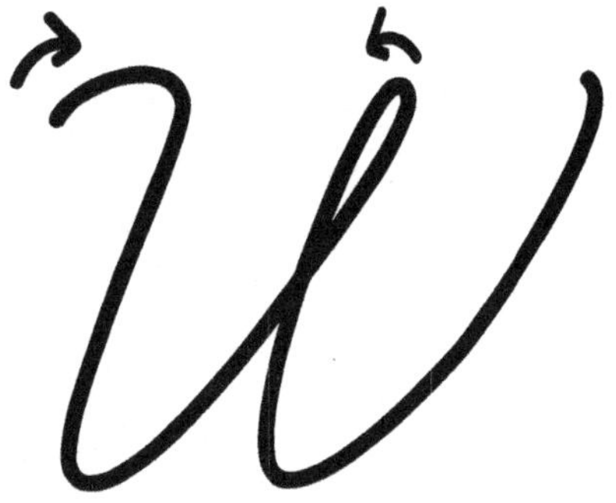

WALRUS

W is for Walrus

Walrus

Walrus Walrus

walrus walrus

Practice page

Practice page

LETTER X

x

x   x   x   x   x   x   x

x

X   X   X   X   X   X

XIPHIAS

X is for Xiphias

Xiphias

Xiphias Xiphias

xiphias xiphias

Practice page

Practice page

LETTER Y

Y   y

y y y y y y y

Y   Y

Y Y Y Y Y Y Y

YAK

Y is for Yak

Yak

Yak Yak Yak Yak

yak yak yak yak

Practice page

Practice page

ZEBRA

Z is for Zebra

Zebra

Zebra Zebra

zebra zebra

Practice page

Practice page

Thank you for choosing Mazing Workbooks
We hope you had a great time!

Please consider leaving a Review.

Made in the USA
Middletown, DE
20 September 2023

38913707R00060